TEAM BUILDING FOR DIVERSE WORK GROUPS

A Practical Guide To Gaining And Sustaining Performance In Diverse Teams

Selma G. Myers

Jossey-Bass
Pfeiffer
San Francisco

RICHARD
CHANG
ASSOCIATES

Published by

 350 Sansome Street, 5th Floor
San Francisco, California 94104-1342
(415) 433-1740; Fax (415) 433-0499
(800) 274-4434; Fax (800) 569-0443

Visit our website at: www.pfeiffer.com

Printing   10   9   8   7   6   5   4   3   2   1

ACKNOWLEDGMENTS

About The Author

Selma Myers is president of Intercultural Development Inc., a California-based company specializing in diversity workshops, seminars, and training for industrial companies, universities, financial institutions, utilities, health care firms, government departments, trade associations, and other organizations.

She is co-author of seven publications in *"The Diversity At Work Training Series,"* and has lived and worked in Europe, South America, and Asia.

The author would like to acknowledge the support of the entire team of professionals at Richard Chang Associates, Inc. for their contribution to the guidebook development process. In addition, special thanks are extended to the many client organizations who have helped to shape the practical ideas and proven methods shared in this guidebook.

Additional Credits

Reviewer:	Keith Kelly
Graphic Layout:	Christina Slater
Cover Design:	John Odam Design Associates

PREFACE

The 1990's have already presented individuals and organizations with some very difficult challenges to face and overcome. So who will have the advantage as we move toward the year 2000 and beyond?

The advantage will belong to those with a commitment to continuous learning. Whether on an individual basis or as an entire organization, one key ingredient to building a continuous learning environment is *The Practical Guidebook Collection* brought to you by the Publications Division of Richard Chang Associates, Inc.

After understanding the future *"learning needs"* expressed by our clients and other potential customers, we are pleased to publish *The Practical Guidebook Collection*. These guidebooks are designed to provide you with proven, *"real-world"* tips, tools, and techniques— on a wide range of subjects—that you can apply in the workplace and/or on a personal level immediately.

Once you've had a chance to benefit from *The Practical Guidebook Collection*, please share your feedback with us. We've included a brief *Evaluation and Feedback Form* at the end of the guidebook that you can fax to us at (714) 756-0853.

With your feedback, we can continuously improve the resources we are providing through the Publications Division of Richard Chang Associates, Inc.

Wishing you successful reading,

Richard Y. Chang
President and CEO
Richard Chang Associates, Inc.

TABLE OF CONTENTS

"A house divided against itself cannot stand."

Abraham Lincoln

CHAPTER ONE

INTRODUCTION

Employee teams have become a way of business life, replacing long-standing management structures. Companies recognize that motivated employees can accomplish more by working as a team, setting their own goals, and developing ways to reach them.

One major issue affecting today's teams is the changing demographics in the workplace. This new work force is made up of more women, immigrants, minorities, and older workers, reflecting the shifting population in our society as a whole.

Some of today's team members may have been born in another country, while others are native-born but are still heavily influenced by their ethnic backgrounds. Others may face barriers because of race, gender, disabilities, life styles, etc.

Unfortunately, the effect of diversity on a team can introduce obstacles to a successful operation. Differences may go unrecognized and get in the way of solid team effort. Indeed, the very idea of a team with so many differences may be uncomfortable to some employees. Such diversity brings new challenges.

Why Read This Guidebook?

It's little wonder that the presence of diversity on a team, where employees have their own perceptions, expectations, and values, can become a touchy problem.

This guidebook is designed to help diverse teams become aware of and understand diversity, and learn to deal with it. The objective is to avoid potential problems and bring cohesiveness to the group.

Research has shown that diverse teams can produce:

- ♦ A wider pool of skills from which to draw
- ♦ Increased creativity
- ♦ Better decision making
- ♦ An exciting mix of ideas from different perspectives

But these advantages and benefits of diversity in a team are not always easy to achieve. It takes a proactive approach, hard work, and a clear commitment to diversity as a core strength, rather than seeing it as a *"problem"* to be overcome.

This guidebook sets out a game plan team leaders and team members can use to take a proactive approach. Use it as a guide to help your team create and sustain high performance, building on the strengths and contributions of a diverse team make-up.

Team members will find that when they begin to understand diversity and learn skills to deal with it, there will be a significant payoff!

Who Should Read This Guidebook?

Managers, supervisors, and team leaders will find this guidebook helpful. Indeed, any employee who is a member of an existing team, or in the process of forming one, will benefit as well.

Since teams have become such an important part of the business world, members should make every effort to overcome any roadblocks to success. It is important to explore how diversity impacts a team so that differences can be understood and appreciated. Each member of the team can then contribute to the fullest.

Remember, diversity ought not stand in the way, but instead translate into a real advantage. You will learn how to avoid the pitfalls diversity can bring, and how to break down barriers, stereotypes, and obstacles arising from unfamiliar ideas, values, and practices.

When And How To Use It

This book is not intended to be a substitute guide for making the transition to a high performance team. It does, however, focus directly on the ways in which diversity affects the transition, the teams, and the team members themselves.

The awareness and skills brought out in this guidebook can be put to use during any stage of the team-building process, starting with the early formation of the team, continuing with growth and development phases, and also applying when there are changes in the team's membership.

Use it in scheduled team development and training sessions, as pre-reading, and/or as a key in-class reference. Have it handy during regular team meetings.

The issues presented in this guidebook, and the techniques to address them, have all been drawn from *"real-life"* experiences, so use the guidebook to help deal with similar situations your team may run into. And lastly, make sure every team member has a chance to read the guidebook and put into practice the lessons learned from it.

For further reading and training resource material on the topic of workplace diversity, please see the entire Workplace Diversity Series of guidebooks (*five titles*) of which this book is part. The lead or *"parent"* guidebook in the series, *Capitalizing On Workplace Diversity*, presents an overall approach and model for an organization or work group to succeed with its diversity as one of its core strengths.

One element of this overall model, building work force capability, is expanded upon in detail in the other three guidebooks in the series, *Successful Staffing In A Diverse Workplace, Communicating In A Diverse Workplace,* and *Tools For Valuing Diversity*. Each of these guidebooks presents a platform from which employees can improve their skills and further develop the competencies needed to contribute to the success of a diverse organization. The guidebooks can be used individually (*in a self-study environment*), or they can be used in a facilitated group setting, as is the case with *Team Building For Diverse Work Groups*.

The Organizational Diversity Success Model™

1

**Create A
Diversity Vision**

Create Your Vision

Determine And
Define Your Values

Promote Your Vision
And Values

4

**Reinforce On An
Ongoing Basis**

Formalize Norms And
Establish Ground Rules

Track And Measure
Your Success

Emphasize Management
Involvement

Capitalizing On
Workplace Diversity

2

**Build Organizational
Awareness And
Commitment**

Assess Where You Are

Take Action On Areas
For Improvement

Focus On Awareness

Tools For Valuing
Diversity

3

**Ensure Work Force
Capability**

Staff For Success

Build Team
Capability

Communicate
Effectively

Successful Staffing In
A Diverse Workplace

Communicating In A
Diverse Workplace

Team Building For
Diverse Work Groups

THE IMPACT OF DIVERSITY ON TEAMS

This guidebook is about teams, about diversity within those teams, and about the challenges that diversity brings. The make-up of the work force is constantly changing, with increasing percentages of women, people of color, and immigrants. However, the term *"diversity"* has now been expanded to include other clusters of people such as those with disabilities, different sexual orientation, various religious backgrounds, alternate life styles, etc. This focus on diversity is a reaction to the evolving population mix. There are few other countries where so many people, coming from so many diverse backgrounds, have to work together under one roof, and especially on teams. This increasingly diverse workplace has truly created new challenges.

There were times in our history when it was expected that the country would become one overall, undifferentiated culture, and that people who were different from the norm would change and *"become like everyone else."*

This thought was described as the *"melting pot"* theory. However, people are beginning to explore another possibility that various groups have a great deal to contribute and can still retain and even celebrate their differences. Nonetheless, in the workplace there are still many demands on the job that require a certain degree of conformity. This is where a team must meet the challenge.

What Is Diversity?

"Diversity" can best be described in terms of differences from the accepted mainstream population, differences such as:

◆ Race	◆ Sexual orientation
◆ Gender	◆ Parental status
◆ Age	◆ Geographic origin
◆ Language	◆ Religion
◆ Disability	◆ Ethnic group
◆ Culture	

... and *any* difference that is irrelevant to one's success in the organization.

One of the major areas of difficulty in dealing with diversity is how people react to differences. In most cases, people's responses have already been imprinted since early childhood, based on a wide range of influences.

When team members start to realize how strongly some of these influences shape ideas about other people, awareness begins. Awareness then leads to greater understanding, and ultimately, the potential to build a positive environment.

Types Of Teams

A functioning team is extremely complex. It involves jointly setting and defining goals, establishing roles, making decisions, developing a plan, and carrying it out. There are several different types of teams operating in the workplace. The type employed in any given situation is determined by the team's objective. The various categories of groups/teams form a continuum, ranging from traditional management-led groups at the left, to fully self-managed teams at the right.

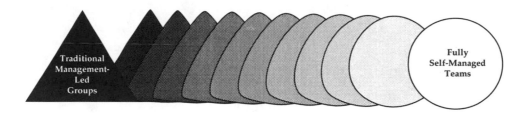

Some of the categories and specific types of teams are:

A. Traditional work groups—a department or other structure in which people work on common work processes (*Natural work group teams*)

B. Impromptu short-term teams—teams intended to operate for a limited time, correct a serious emergency situation, and then disband (*SWAT teams*)

C. Special purpose teams—teams intended to address a process improvement, undertake a project, solve a short-term problem, and then disband (*process improvement teams, project teams, or problem-solving teams*)

D. Cross-functional teams—teams intended to bring together individuals from different work groups

E. Self-managed teams—teams empowered with the authority to manage ongoing work processes or a full department (*also referred to as self-directed teams*)

As a general rule, the farther to the right a team appears on the continuum below, the greater the interaction between members, and the greater the need is for *"teamwork"* and interpersonal skills.

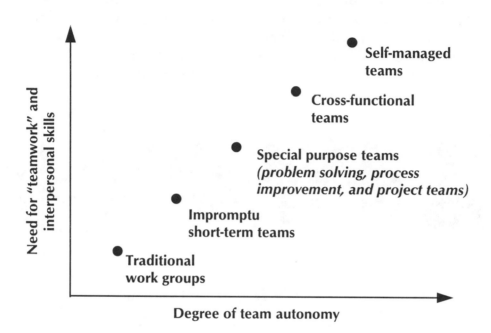

Cultural Differences And Types Of Teams

"Culture" is only one of the differences that diversity brings, but it would be helpful at this point to look at culture. We can examine cultural differences and determine ourselves how they would affect the five types of teams.

"Culture" involves the rules people live by as passed down from generation to generation. It also includes attitudes, values, communication styles, patterns of thinking, and behavior.

Cultural differences often play a role in the way team members interact with one another. It is the cultural aspect of diversity that team members should begin to be aware of.

Here are some aspects of culture that determine how people respond in team activities:

- ◆ Formality versus informality
- ◆ Independence versus dependence
- ◆ Direct versus indirect communication
- ◆ Competition versus harmony
- ◆ Risk-taking versus risk-avoidance
- ◆ Time and time consciousness
- ◆ Rewards and recognition
- ◆ Perceptions and assumptions
- ◆ Challenge of authority
- ◆ Individual versus group orientation

Look at the types of teams and consider which aspects of cultural differences listed above might have the greatest effect on each type. Following is a list of the types of teams, along with one aspect of culture which would strongly affect each. These choices are subjective, and in many cases, others could be just as valid.

Traditional work groups
Formality versus informality—where the long-term nature of the team calls for relaxed interpersonal relations, which is uncomfortable for some groups whose tradition leans towards formality.

Impromptu teams
Time and time consciousness—where immediate action is necessary and people from different backgrounds may respond differently to time constraints and the decision-making process.

Special purpose teams
Risk-taking versus risk-avoidance—where people from some groups can more easily accept uncertainty and take risks in weighing downside versus upside consequences.

Cross-functional teams
Individual versus group orientation—where people from certain groups are *"we" (rather than "I")* oriented and put the group's mission ahead of their individual needs.

Self-managed teams
Individual versus group orientation—when individual needs for centralized authority and control have to give way to democratic *"team"* decision-making and management.

You may find other diversity issues, such as biases, stereotyping, and communication, showing up in any type of team. However, as your team matures and continues to function, the building of relationships between team members becomes even more important. The key element is that members understand and appreciate the value that each individual brings to the team, regardless of differences.

Identifying Barriers To Team Effectiveness

When a diverse team is formed, a number of factors come into play. Some may become barriers to personal interaction and, eventually, to team performance. Among these factors are:

- Discomfort with differences
- Stereotypes
- Biases against the unfamiliar
- Language differences
- Cultural baggage

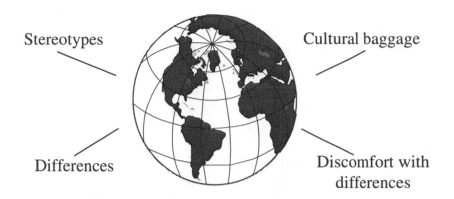

Stereotypes

Cultural baggage

Differences

Discomfort with differences

When a new, diverse team is being formed, members who might have barely known each other suddenly find themselves face-to-face and having to work closely together. Here are some examples of how the above factors might impact team performance.

Discomfort with differences

Members of one team were initially uncomfortable with a team member who was in a wheelchair. They were unsure of how to treat him. They wanted to be helpful but did not know whether to openly address his disability, assist him at every turn, or wait for him to ask for help. Above all, they wanted to show concern and compassion, but underneath they were not certain of what he could accomplish. They suspected that they would have to help him at every turn.

Some team members automatically assigned nonexistent disabilities to him. They modified their behavior accordingly, such as physically helping when he didn't need it, or even speaking patronizingly, such as raising their voices as if he were hearing-impaired.

This early discomfort with differences could have resulted in his partial exclusion from certain activities or events, discouraging him and consequently reducing the valuable contributions he might otherwise have made.

Stereotypes

When a new team meets, without realizing it, members may rely on stereotypes to form opinions about others based on what they initially see.

For example, one team member was from a highly visible minority group. She was born in America, grew up in the Northwest, and spoke accent-free English. When asked, she stated that the greatest influence on her life was *"Oregon."*

At that first meeting, however, based on stereotypes, some of the team members were sure she was a foreigner and would be difficult to communicate with. They believed that she was not familiar with the American way of life and would hold back the rest of the members.

Biases against the unfamiliar

There was one technically competent employee who happened to be from a minority group. He would be working on a team where some of the others had rarely known or worked with people of color.

These people could be biased and fear that he would have a different perspective on the issues even though there was no evidence to that effect.

If the biases were allowed to prevail, he would be treated differently than the other team members, tension would result, and team efficiency would be affected.

Language differences

A middle-aged foreign-born production engineer had impressive skills in his field and had even taught the subject at a prestigious university in his native country. Though he was knowledgeable about English, he was still very hard to understand and was not always able to express himself clearly.

His language limitations were often interpreted as a lack of engineering knowledge and skills. Some team members felt that this language limitation disrupted the team effort, demanding extra effort by the other members.

Cultural baggage

Just as many people carry an attaché case, a newspaper, or an umbrella to work, so do they take their cultural baggage. In this *"baggage"* they bring, for example, their attitudes about people who are different, their ideas about how people should treat one another, their perspectives on time, and their outlook on work in general.

These attitudes and ideas are often so firmly fixed that they are difficult to change. However, in today's business world, the flexibility to deal with change is vital to survival.

Your cultural baggage has been packed over the years. For some, it may be as large as a foot locker; for others, as small as a backpack. Think about your own cultural baggage and how it might be a barrier when it comes to being a member of a team.

Overcoming Barriers

As you can see, team members' responses to differences can create barriers. Some members of the group may feel discomfort with differences, carry their culture baggage into the workplace, view other as stereotypes, and let biases get in the way. Inability to resolve language issues can also damage team cohesiveness.

Overcoming these barriers is the key to building a successful, diverse work team. The differences mentioned above are based on perceptions, stereotypes, and *"baggage"* we carry with us. But other differences between team members, when addressed in a positive manner, add to team strength and success.

In the next chapter, you will read about a model with four key elements that can help overcome potential barriers to building a high performance team.

CHAPTER TWO WORKSHEET:
THE IMPACT OF DIVERSITY ON YOUR TEAM

1. Pinpoint where your team lies on the continuum of the different types of teams *(see page 10)*. How does this *"positioning"* relate to the issues of diversity on the team?

_____

_____

_____

_____

a. How might the issues change if the team were to move to the right on the continuum?

_____

_____

_____

b. To the left?

_____

_____

_____

2. Which of the following have acted as barriers to your team's improved effectiveness? How? *(Jot down a specific example you can share with other team members.)*

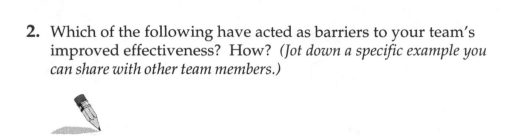

a) Discomfort with differences
Example:

_____

_____

b) Stereotypes
Example:

_____

_____

c) Biases against the unfamiliar
Example:

_____

_____

d) Language differences
Example:

_____

_____

e) Cultural baggage
Example:

_____

_____

3. How has your team overcome these issues in the past?

_____

_____

_____

_____

_____

_____

_____

4. What additional ideas do you have for your team to overcome these potential barriers?

_____

_____

_____

_____

_____

_____

_____

A MODEL FOR A HIGH PERFORMANCE DIVERSE TEAM

Models are very helpful in illustrating the fundamental structure of a business system. Our model will give you an idea of the ingredients required to build a diverse high performance team.

Four Key Factors

The model illustrates four key factors needed for diverse teams to succeed.

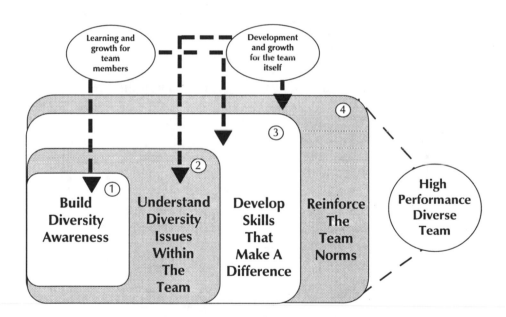

We will examine each of these key factors and how they operate to produce a well-functioning team, with diversity taken into account.

Build Diversity Awareness

Why is diversity awareness important? Before you can work with other people in a high performance team, you have to know something about yourself. Awareness means the recognition of what is important to you as an individual and your values, perceptions, and expectations.

Awareness of diversity goes beyond just looking at differences. It also means that you are obligated to:

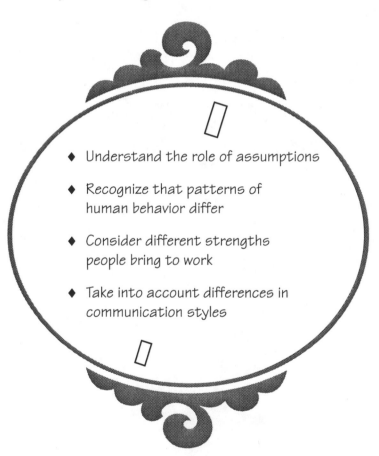

- ◆ Understand the role of assumptions

- ◆ Recognize that patterns of human behavior differ

- ◆ Consider different strengths people bring to work

- ◆ Take into account differences in communication styles

As a team member, you need to know something about these factors, not only as they relate to you, but to your fellow team members as well.

Understand Diversity Issues Within The Team

In any high performance team, all members need to be knowledgeable about:

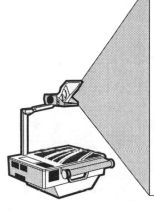

♦ The type and mission of the team

♦ Roles and responsibilities of each individual

♦ Individual strengths of other team members

♦ Open lines of communication

However, diverse teams require a deeper level of awareness. For example, there may be one member with limited language skills. During the discussion of the team mission, that individual might not fully understand, but would hesitate to say so for fear of losing face. The result? That member's contribution to the team effort and comprehension of the mission may not be what it could be.

This situation, and others like it, call for an understanding of the critical types of issues impacting diverse teams:

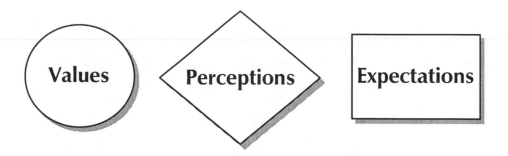

Develop Interpersonal Skills That Make A Difference

In a diverse team, the skills needed to perform effectively require members to:

♦ Develop strategic communication—listening and responding

♦ Treat each person as an individual

♦ Test accuracy of assumptions

♦ Resolve conflicts

Listening and Responding

Listening and Responding

As explained earlier, developing open lines of communication is extremely important. Each member of a team needs to feel valued; your active listening and appropriate responses contribute greatly to building relationships.

One of the biggest barriers to personal interaction is incorrect assumptions. Without checking assumptions and testing their accuracy, team members can misunderstand, misinterpret, and indeed, miss the entire point, often leading to conflict.

Conflict occurs in most teams and is usually considered counterproductive. Conflict can also have a positive effect, and when handled well, can produce creative ideas and help team members learn together and work together.

Reinforce The Team Norms

Team norms are the conventional standards (*both "formal" and "informal"*) by which teams conduct themselves. Some examples are:

- ◆ Shared goals

- ◆ Team practices understood/ accepted

- ◆ Group support roles/ responsibilities acknowledged

- ◆ Ground rules

When there is diversity on the team, norms become crucial. Some members from diverse groups may find that norms which are readily acceptable to other team members are difficult to accept. For example, if one member comes from a group that is highly competitive, he may find that submerging his own ideas to the will of the group goes against his grain. Conflict arises.

So far, in the course of this guidebook, you have already read short examples about how different people face situations where the nature of their diversity affected the way others treated them.

These situations came from team experiences at Chester Cylinder Corp. In the remaining chapters, we will explore more thoroughly diversity-sensitive issues at Chester and the ways in which they came to light and/or were handled.

Chester Cylinder Case

Chester Cylinder Corp....

is a 180-employee company that builds hydraulic cylinders. Chester has decided to introduce self-managed teams, with the pilot program assigned to the Miniature Products Department. This department was recently expanded, had new people brought in, and now has twelve members performing machining, assembly, quality control, testing, and production engineering.

Each subgroup has a Lead Operator who handles limited supervisory tasks. The work ranges from semi-skilled to highly skilled. The department is multicultural, with four female and eight male employees, and one employee who operates from a wheelchair.

It is the company's intention to modify the Miniature Products Department into an established team.

♦ The machining subgroup operates semi-automatic equipment, some numeri-cally-controlled, to machine tubes, rods, end-caps, and mounts.

♦ The assembly group assembles the machined components into finished miniature cylinders.

♦ Quality Control conducts inspections to assure that the machined parts are to specification.

♦ The Testers check the cylinders for leak integrity, alignment, fit, and final visual inspection.

♦ The Production Engineer monitors the production processes and designs and installs improvements to make them more efficient.

We will look at the formation and operation of the group as a team, paying special attention to the impact of diversity.

Personnel—Chester Cylinder Corp., Miniature Products Department

Individual	Assignment
* Gordon	Machinist
Charlie	Machinist
Lucy	Machinist
* Tony	Assembler
Mai Lin	Assembler
Bob	Assembler
Doris	Assembler
Juan	Quality Control
Roger	Quality Control
* Darnell	Tester
Severina	Tester
Loc Nam	Production Engineer

* Lead Operator

Five department members are not white Anglos. One white Anglo uses a wheelchair.

Self-Managed Team

Traditional Work Groups

In the chapters to come, follow the department as it undertakes a transition from a traditional department structure to that of a self-managed team. Instead of being directed solely by a manager, formulating plans and making decisions become group processes. The focus is on the impact of diversity during the transition. For more information on self-managed teams, please read the guide-book *Succeeding As A Self-Managed Team.*

CHAPTER THREE WORKSHEET: DEVELOPING YOUR HIGH PERFORMANCE DIVERSE TEAM

1. What specific learning opportunities do you see for your team and its members in each of the four elements of the High Performance Diverse Team model?

a) **Build Diversity Awareness**
Learning opportunities for team members:

_____

_____

_____

_____

_____

b) **Understand Diversity Issues Within The Team**
Development and growth for the team itself:

_____

_____

_____

_____

_____

c) **Develop Skills That Make A Difference**
Learning opportunities for team members:

_____

_____

_____

_____

_____

_____

_____

_____

d) **Reinforce The Team Norms**
Development and growth for the team itself:

_____

_____

_____

_____

_____

_____

_____

_____

BUILD DIVERSITY AWARENESS

In a high performance diverse team, members' awareness of themselves and others is very important. People cannot deal effectively with diversity without understanding their own values and beliefs. They can then develop an awareness that other people come from different backgrounds, with different life experiences, and in fact, operate from different points of view.

Furthermore, it is equally important that team members recognize that they share similarities as well as differences.

In pursuing diversity awareness, consider the following:

- ◆ Patterns of behavior by diverse members
- ◆ Patterns of others' behavior toward diverse members
- ◆ Distinct strengths various members contribute
- ◆ Differences in communication styles

Building diversity awareness among team members involves two distinct elements: self-assessment and team analysis.

Self-Assessment

Self-assessment means exploring your own values, perceptions, and expectations. Team members need to look at these and how they relate to their own behavior toward differences. For example, your feelings and actions could range from blatant hostility to complete acceptance. It is therefore important that all team members examine their own points of view regarding people who are different.

One approach to a diversity self-assessment employs a simple four-step process:

1. Examine your first responses to someone who is different

2. Review your specific assumptions about the other person

3. Check the reality behind your assumptions

4. Find commonalities/build trust

For example, note the following illustration of how this four-step approach resolved one issue at Chester Cylinder.

At the first team meeting ...

Roger learns that he will be partnered with Juan, whom he had only just met. He notices the way Juan looks, that he speaks with an accent and smiles frequently. But the only people like Juan that Roger had ever known were all gardeners or day laborers, and he was not comfortable with the idea of having to depend on Juan.

However, Roger had recently gone through a training session which addressed diversity issues. After thinking it over, he realized that he was letting his first impressions get in the way, and he proceeded to assess himself by using the Diversity Self-Assessment Planner.

Having found some common interests, Roger lets Juan know that they have a lot in common. He is aware that building trust takes a long time, but at least both of them have made a good start.

As rapport and trust are being established, Roger feels a lot better and learns to his surprise that Juan had also had his own preset notions about Roger. With this initial self-assessment on both parts, some of the barriers have been removed and progress has been made. Now they can build a relationship, and it will be easier for them to depend on one another from here on....

Does self-assessment really work? At the end of this chapter you will have a chance to test your ability to assess your own openness to diversity. You may be surprised at the results.

Diversity Self-Assessment Planner™

1. Examine your first responses to someone who is different

Roger realizes that he is judging his new partner on appearance, language, and his own stereotype: which are simply the first assumptions he made.

4. Find commonalities, build trust

Roger also begins to look for things that he and Juan have in common and learns that Juan is knowledgeable about sports statistics and has been working at Chester for four years. He also discovers that they drive the same make and model car.

2. Review your specific assumptions about the other person

Roger assumes that Juan will be happy-go-lucky rather than serious, have a poor time sense, and will not be dependable.

3. Check the reality behind your assumptions

Roger proceeds to have a discussion with Juan, in the course of which he learns that Juan is a family man, diligent, ambitious, and attends college at night.

A week after Roger and Juan had cleared the air...

Roger is having coffee in the cafeteria. He tells Bob, Doris, and Tony about his conversation with Juan. Tony then admits that the three of them have been concerned about the two Testers, Darnell and Severina. They have heard that many Testers in other departments do a good job, but they are unsure of how these two will perform.

Roger says, *"Think about it, guys, you may be stereotyping two entire groups of people at one time. It sounds like you're not working from personal knowledge about Darnell and Severina, but just from your own thoughts about people who are different from you."*

Since one of the team goals is to treat people as individuals and with respect, their assessment of themselves and their behavior needs to be looked at. Roger reminds them about his talk with Juan and the four steps he had learned in his diversity training.

In the cafeteria a week later, Roger again meets Bob, Doris, and Tony, and the subject of differences comes up again. He learns that the three of them have thought over what he said and agreed to hold back any judgment of the Testers, at least until they actually see how both Darnell and Severina perform....

So far, we have talked about personal self-assessment, which should be taking place constantly to avoid falling back into negative patterns. Yet, self-assessment is only one part of awareness, because the team itself plays a role in the total diversity awareness picture. Now let's consider the entire team.

Team Analysis

Every team needs to review and evaluate its ongoing dynamics, especially diverse teams—in other words, a *"Team Analysis."* One way to do this is through the use of a formal team diversity assessment process. Check the appropriate box using the scale where (1) = Strongly disagree, (2) = Disagree, (3) = Neither agree or disagree, (4) Agree, and (5) = Strongly agree.

TEAM DIVERSITY ASSESSMENT

		1	2	3	4	5
1.	Our team has a stated vision.					
2.	The vision is accepted by all.					
3.	The vision is understood by all.					
4.	It includes reference to diversity.					
5.	It considers the values and needs of each of its members.					
6.	Our team environment supports diversity.					
7.	Our team encourages members to be open with one another.					
8.	Team members help one another.					
9.	Our team promotes the sharing of success.					
10.	Our team encourages individual interaction across diversity lines.					
11.	The team members are open to differences of opinion.					
12.	There is appreciation of the talents and skills of each individual.					
13.	Members can count on one another, irrespective of their diverse backgrounds.					
14.	The team is able to deal with interpersonal problems and conflicts.					
15.	Team members feel secure in bringing up problems and conflicts.					
16.	The team members can determine whether their problems are diversity-related.					
17.	There is a system in place for addressing problems and conflicts.					

Scoring Key

81 to 85 – Excellent

Congratulations! Your team has successfully integrated diversity awareness into the team's values and operating norms, making it possible to capitalize on each other's differences. You should try to share the lessons learned from your team's experiences with other groups in your organization that may not be as far along.

75 to 80 –Very good

Your team is making progress and has all the ingredients for even greater success. Focus on the areas which received lower scores from team members. Address these areas with the entire team to find out what can be done to improve. Develop specific action plans and take the team assessment again in a month or two to track your improvement.

61 to 75 – Room for improvement

Your team has some core strengths but clearly there are areas for growth and improvement. Review the areas that received the lowest scores and put them on the agenda at the next team meeting. At the same time, look at one or two areas that received the highest scores and have the team focus on how these strengths have been achieved. There may be some cues for building the other areas. Set specific targets for areas to improve and agree on a plan to get there. *(You may find the companion guidebook in this series, Tools For Valuing Diversity, an ideal resource for further team development.)* Make sure the team recognizes the advantages of improving—that there will be a greater sense of teamwork and harmony, as well as better work performance overall. Set a specific date for the next team assessment and for a follow-up analysis of the results at that time.

60 or less – Oops, problems ahead!

Your team may already be running into problems. The team assessment provides you with a starting point on which to focus. Pick one or two specific areas that received low scores on the assessment and focus your team's efforts there. Don't try to accomplish everything overnight. Instead, plan for progress in small steps, retaking the assessment test as the team progresses. Even though a journey of small steps can seem like a marathon when you are standing at the starting line, the destination makes every step worthwhile. Think about bringing in an outside facilitator to help your team start moving toward being a high performing diverse work team.

At Chester Cylinder...

the team soon learned dramatically the importance of diversity issues in handling internal problems.

Shortly after the Miniature Products Department began the transition from a department to a team structure, the first crisis occurred. The company's best customer had rejected a large shipment of 1/2" bore cylinders, claiming that they leaked oil past the piston. Immediately a team meeting was called.

Even before all the facts were in, finger pointing began and subgroups started blaming the problem on each other. Among the charges were:

✖ *"Female Machinists never could read a micrometer properly, so naturally a mistake was made by machining."*

✖ One team member had spotted the potential problem ahead of time, but was unwilling to bring it up for fear of *"making waves."*

 "It takes too much strength for a woman to assemble stiff lock rings in a tight barrel."

✖ *"After the Production Engineer revised a procedure for using the out-of-round inspection fixture, he did not clearly explain the new instructions for Quality Control."*

✖ One Tester was constantly held to a lower testing standard purely because of his race, so *"He got away with passing defective units."*

✖ Because he was in a wheelchair, one Assembler used a different assembly procedure from the other Assemblers, so *"His units were probably the defective ones."*

Two team members suggested that they not jump to conclusions but wait for an engineering analysis of the rejects. A second team meeting was scheduled for the next day.

Meanwhile, however, the meeting went on to look into the specific charges. They were all proven to be baseless.

✔ The female Machinist's rejection rate was not excessive, but evenly matched those of the male machinists. Micrometer readings had never been a problem for her.

✔ The employee who was unwilling to mention the potential problem was from a culture that valued group harmony over disunity. It was explained to the employee that group harmony would be more seriously damaged if possible problems were **not** reported. The employee realized how important it was to report any problems in the future and agreed to try to do so.

✔ Before taking on the assembly job, the female employee had been tested in the entire assembly process, including strength, and was found to be just as capable as male employees. *(Indeed, she exceeded them in dexterity.)* Furthermore, the Production Engineer offered to design and build an assembly fixture which reduced the strength required, thus avoiding Assembler fatigue.

✔ The Production Engineer, aware of his communication limitations, had also issued new written instructions for the use of the out-of-round inspection fixture, which were posted next to that fixture.

✔ Some team members who had worked in other departments reported that the performance and output of the team's Testers were in line with those of other Testers in the company, and the Tester in question was entitled to be measured by the same standard as the others.

✔ There was no credible evidence that the unconventional procedure used by the Assembler in the wheelchair caused rejects.

The team concluded that they had been too hasty in their assumptions, which in every case were completely false. Several members pointed out that what they had just gone through had taught them a lesson, and they would have to analyze themselves as a team to be sure that:

◆ The team vision would include diversity

◆ The team environment would support diversity

◆ The team would encourage individual interaction across diversity lines

◆ The team would be able to deal with interpersonal problems and conflicts

At the next day's meeting, the engineers reported that the leak problem was caused by one supplier's slightly off-specification seal, which did not leak until after several hours of use. It was clear that the charges leveled at various team members were not valid and instead were based on stereotypes among the team members.

The team decided to complete the Team Diversity Assessment, and found that their score had improved from 63, when they completed it the first time, to 75. *"I think working through this problem together brought a lot of issues to the surface and helped us improve the way we will work together from now on,"* suggested Mai Lin. The rest of the group nodded their agreement as they prepared to tackle the work order plans for the coming week.

CHAPTER FOUR WORKSHEET:
BUILDING YOUR TEAM'S DIVERSITY
AWARENESS

1. Have each team member complete the Diversity Self-
    Assessment Planner for their first response to another team
    member. *(Note: You can copy and use the blank form in the
    Appendix.)* Then, have the team members present and discuss
    the conclusions of their completed Planner to the other team
    member. Finally, have each member write down their lessons
    learned and be prepared to discuss them at the next team
    meeting.

    Lessons learned:

    _____

    _____

    _____

    _____

    _____

    _____

    _____

    _____

    _____

    _____

2. Have each team member complete the Team Diversity Assessment questionnaire. Combine their scores to come up with an average score for the team. Use the scoring guide to help the team select an appropriate course of action. *(Note: You can copy and use the blank form in the Appendix.)*

Our course of action:

_____

_____

_____

_____

_____

_____

_____

3. Based on the average team score in the Team Diversity Assessment questionnaire, and the areas on which the team will focus to improve, agree on a firm date the team will take the Assessment again to gauge its progress.

Date first taken: _____

Follow-up date: _____

DIVERSITY ISSUES WITHIN THE TEAM

By now, your self-assessment and team analysis have strengthened your diversity awareness. Your next step is to go beyond awareness and explore the issues that impact diverse teams. An understanding of these issues will help you and your team appreciate the differences in others.

The issues usually fall into one or more of the following three categories:

- ♦ Values
- ♦ Perceptions
- ♦ Expectations

Taken together, these issues, or forces, represent important aspects of *"culture,"* through which each diverse group has its own shared experiences and rules to live by. Learning about the cultures of various diverse groups can help you understand and appreciate *"What makes different people tick,"* and lead to better team performance.

Understand Differences In Others

As a team member, you must constantly deal with others whose culture may differ considerably from your own.

When you meet other team members for the first time, you can only base your impression on their physical appearance, facial features, skin color, hair, stature, dress, etc.

However, in working together, you must learn to know others on a deeper level and not be influenced by first impressions only. You may find yourself facing behaviors that seem difficult to understand. Here is where knowledge of cultural diversity can make you more comfortable with differences in others.

Consider the various ways diversity can impact a team. One approach is to examine a Team Development Model consisting of five stages. Think about the possible ways diversity could affect each stage of the team development process.

Team Development Model

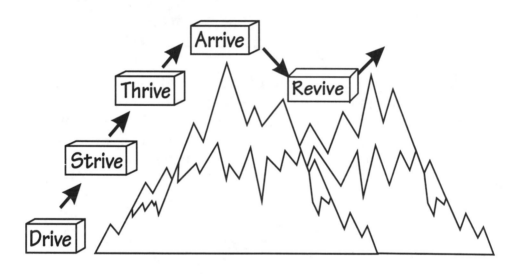

 **Drive**   *"Driving"*—Focusing on mission, goals, priorities, and guidelines.

However, while some cultural groups are comfortable in a structured environment, other groups may not be. Still other groups have different levels of English comprehension and different cultural attitudes towards time.

Strive

"Striving"—Moving ahead with full understanding and agreement on roles and responsibilities.

However, some cultural groups have a great interest in gaining more responsibility, while others are not as open to taking on responsibility without formal support such as rank, age, etc. Some individuals may be very open to the concept of change while others are satisfied with the status quo.

Thrive

"Thriving"—Rapid growth involving peer feedback, conflict management, and decision making.

However, various cultural groups may have very different approaches to communication and conflict, and reach decisions in a number of different ways. For example, certain cultures value directness and frankness in interpersonal communication, while others place a high value on subtlety in their communication style.

Arrive

"Arriving" —Peak performance, where all the factors are in sync.

Finally, the team has arrived when all members have been recognized, appreciated, accepted, encouraged, and acknowledged for the strengths they bring to the team.

Revive

"Reviving" —Regaining peak performance when slippage in team performance occurs, or when team membership changes.

The interaction between members of a diverse team needs to be reexamined when the team membership changes, or when there is a change in the team's mandate or purpose. Blaming, without recognizing cultural differences, is counterproductive. Instead, members will remain open-minded and motivate and support each other to attain peak performance again.

Now let's return to the three principal forces of diversity in light of their impact on diverse work teams.

Different aspects of these three forces of diversity come into play throughout the team-building process from the *"Driving"* phase all the way through the *"Reviving"* phase. The key to ongoing team success is to be able to identify and deal with the issues as they come up, or even to be proactive and address them before they come up, as part of the team formation and team learning process. One approach your team can take is to have all members *"position"* themselves on the spectrum from left to right for each of the individual points or perspectives within the *"Values," "Perceptions,"* and *"Expectations"* categories. Have team members pair off to compare and discuss where they position themselves for two or three of the points. *(Note: The following assessment tool is also provided in the Appendix for you to copy and use.)*

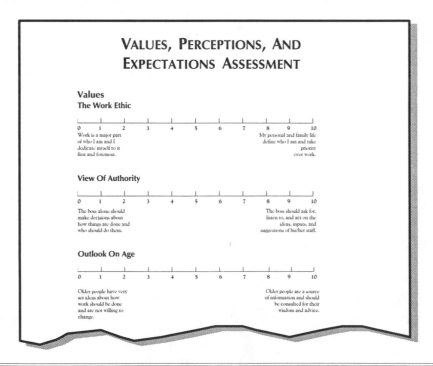

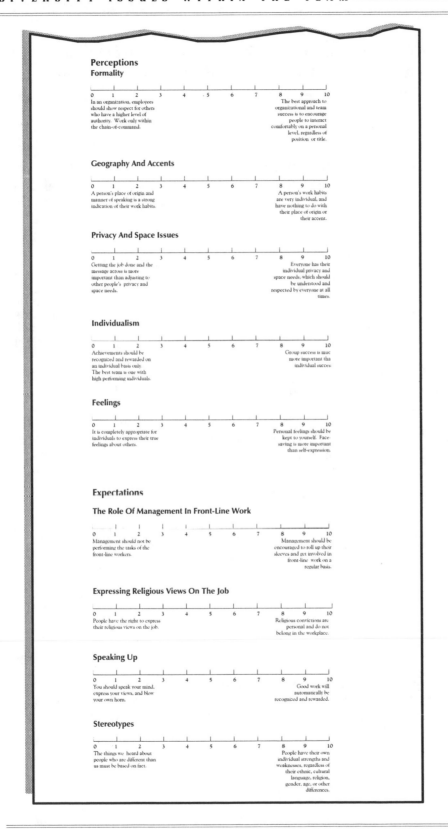

Perceptions
Formality

```
0    1    2    3    4  . 5    6    7    8    9    10
```
In an organization, employees should show respect for others who have a higher level of authority. Work only within the chain-of-command.

The best approach to organizational and team success is to encourage people to interact comfortably on a personal level, regardless of position or title.

Geography And Accents

```
0    1    2    3    4    5    6    7    8    9    10
```
A person's place of origin and manner of speaking is a strong indication of their work habits.

A person's work habits are very individual, and have nothing to do with their place of origin or their accent.

Privacy And Space Issues

```
0    1    2    3    4    5    6    7    8    9    10
```
Getting the job done and the message across is more important than adjusting to other people's privacy and space needs.

Everyone has their individual privacy and space needs, which should be understood and respected by everyone at all times.

Individualism

```
0    1    2    3    4    5    6    7    8    9    10
```
Achievements should be recognized and rewarded on an individual basis only. The best team is one with high performing individuals.

Group success is much more important than individual success.

Feelings

```
0    1    2    3    4    5    6    7    8    9    10
```
It is completely appropriate for individuals to express their true feelings about others.

Personal feelings should be kept to yourself. Face-saving is more important than self-expression.

Expectations

The Role Of Management In Front-Line Work

```
0    1    2    3    4    5    6    7    8    9    10
```
Management should not be performing the tasks of the front-line workers.

Management should be encouraged to roll up their sleeves and get involved in front-line work on a regular basis.

Expressing Religious Views On The Job

```
0    1    2    3    4    5    6    7    8    9    10
```
People have the right to express their religious views on the job.

Religious convictions are personal and do not belong in the workplace.

Speaking Up

```
0    1    2    3    4    5    6    7    8    9    10
```
You should speak your mind, express your views, and blow your own horn.

Good work will automatically be recognized and rewarded.

Stereotypes

```
0    1    2    3    4    5    6    7    8    9    10
```
The things we heard about people who are different than us must be based on fact.

People have their own individual strengths and weaknesses, regardless of their ethnic, cultural, language, religion, gender, age, or other differences.

Then reassign pairs a couple of times so each member has an opportunity to compare his or her *"positions"* with several other team members.

Values

Individuals from various diverse groups may come to the job with different sets of values. A number of these values are work related and can affect the operation of the team. For example:

The Work Ethic

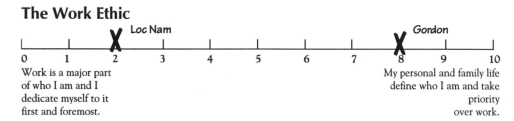

| | | Loc Nam | | | | | | Gordon | |
|0|1|2|3|4|5|6|7|8|9|10|

Work is a major part of who I am and I dedicate myself to it first and foremost.

My personal and family life define who I am and take priority over work.

> ### The work ethic itself...
> Loc Nam thoroughly enjoys designing elegant equipment. He loves his job and even works on a drawing board at home to complete or improve his designs. He measures his worth by the work he does. Gordon is a fine machinist and lead operator but believes there are other things in life besides work. He turns off all job-related thoughts as soon as he leaves the plant.

View Of Authority

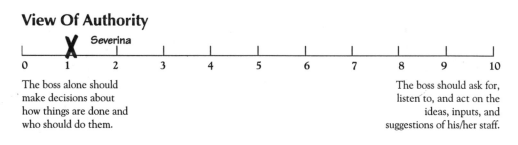

| | Severina | | | | | | | | |
|0|1|2|3|4|5|6|7|8|9|10|

The boss alone should make decisions about how things are done and who should do them.

The boss should ask for, listen to, and act on the ideas, inputs, and suggestions of his/her staff.

> ### View of authority...
> Severina believes that a boss is a boss. She can't understand why the boss asks for her opinion. She expects the boss to know what to do and to tell people when and how to do it. On the other hand, most of her fellow team members are willing to disagree or express their opinions because they feel that their input is as important as his.

Outlook On Age

Team's initial view of Charlie

Former dept's view of Charlie

0   1   2   3   4   5   6   7   8   9   10

Older people have very
set ideas about how
work should be done
and are not willing to
change.

Older people are a source
of information and should
be consulted for their
wisdom and advice.

Outlook on age...

Charlie is considerably older than the others. Some team members perceive
him as boring, stuck in his ways, and unable to accept new ideas. Members of
his former department saw him as more experienced and capable, even going
to him for machining advice.

Individualism

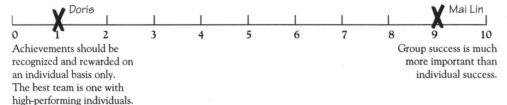

Doris

Mai Lin

0   1   2   3   4   5   6   7   8   9   10

Achievements should be
recognized and rewarded on
an individual basis only.
The best team is one with
high-performing individuals.

Group success is much
more important than
individual success.

Individualism...

Doris has a habit of bragging about her assembly speed and how much
harder she works than anyone else. Mai Lin works equally as fast as Doris but
doesn't brag, because in her culture, group success is much more important
than individual success.

Feelings

A foreign born team member

Tony

0   1   2   3   4   5   6   7   8   9   10

It is completely appropriate for
individuals to express their true
feelings about others.

Personal feelings should be
kept to yourself. Face-
saving is more important
than self-expression.

Feelings...

When it comes to comments about other people's work, Tony is a real believer
in the *"John Wayne School of Communication."* He often blurts out, *"You gotta tell
it like it is!"* Whenever he expresses such an opinion in a team meeting, two of
the foreign-born team members are surprised and annoyed, believing that
personal feelings are important and saving-face is absolutely necessary.

When all members of a diverse team understand how important different cultural values are and show respect, they will be able to build strong team relationships.

Perceptions

Perceptions are the ways people see situations and the distinctive qualities of others. Different cultural groups come to the job with different perceptions that have been imprinted by their early environment and experiences. Perceptions often determine the expectations people have for themselves and for others. For example:

Formality

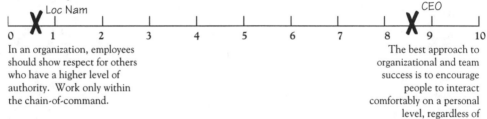

In an organization, employees should show respect for others who have a higher level of authority. Work only within the chain-of-command.

The best approach to organizational and team success is to encourage people to interact comfortably on a personal level, regardless of position or title.

Formality...

Shortly after Loc Nam joined the company, the CEO announced that he would maintain an open door policy and that people should feel free to drop in and call him by his first name. Because Loc Nam came from a culture in which important people were not so approachable and were always addressed by a title and their last name, he was very uncomfortable and avoided speaking directly to the CEO at all.

Geography And Accents

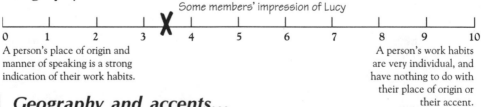

A person's place of origin and manner of speaking is a strong indication of their work habits.

A person's work habits are very individual, and have nothing to do with their place of origin or their accent.

Geography and accents...

Lucy is from Georgia and speaks with a Southern accent. During the team orientation meeting, she was teased about her pronunciation of certain words. Some team members even laughed at her and decided she was a not-too-bright Southerner. It took some time before they became used to her accent and realized that it had nothing to do with her job performance.

Privacy And Space Issues

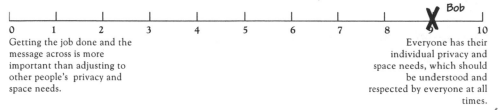

| 0 | 1 | 2 | 3 | 4 | 5 | 6 | 7 | 8 | 9 | 10 |

Getting the job done and the message across is more important than adjusting to other people's privacy and space needs.

Everyone has their individual privacy and space needs, which should be understood and respected by everyone at all times.

> ## *Privacy and space issues...*
> Bob was in a wheelchair and did not like being fussed over. Moreover, he believed his *"space"* extended out beyond his wheelchair and he hated it when people leaned over to talk to him, yelled, or whispered. He often wanted to shout back, *"Just because my legs don't work don't mean my ears are broke!"*

When it comes to perceptions, what you see is not always what you get. People who come from other cultural orientations, people of different ages, gender, and so on, may perceive situations from entirely different perspectives than you do. Pay attention to your own initial perceptions. Perhaps they need to be modified or replaced after you have considered their biases.

After recognizing differences in perceptions, follow up by seeing how they affect your expectations. Note how often stereotyping or limited exposure to differences has had a determining effect. Indeed, your expectations apply not only to others, but to yourself as well.

Expectations

Expectations are another principal force impacting team relationships. Ideas about what we expect from ourselves and what we expect from others are often based on values and perceptions. People also come to their jobs with specific expectations, based on their gender, or religious, cultural, ethnic, or language backgrounds.

These expectations have been filtered and shaped by a person's early environment and experiences. For example:

The Role Of Management In Front-Line Work

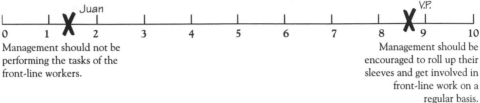

0   1   2   3   4   5   6   7   8   9   10

Management should not be
performing the tasks of the
front-line workers.

Management should be
encouraged to roll up their
sleeves and get involved in
front-line work on a
regular basis.

The role of management in front-line work...

The V.P. of Manufacturing walks through the department one day and stops to chat with Juan. The V.P. sees that Juan needs help in one series of critical measurements, so he rolls up his sleeves and gets involved. When the V.P. leaves, he feels very good about having helped Juan. Juan, however, feels uncomfortable because he would never expect a vice president to do shop work.

Expressing Religious Views On The Job

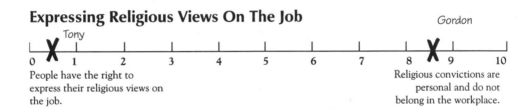

0   1   2   3   4   5   6   7   8   9   10

People have the right to
express their religious views on
the job.

Religious convictions are
personal and do not
belong in the workplace.

Expressing religious views on the job...

Tony has recently developed some very deep religious convictions and has concluded that his church has all the answers. He starts discussing religion at every opportunity, particularly with Gordon, trying to convince him to join his congregation. However, Gordon is very comfortable with his own religious beliefs. Though Gordon has always believed strongly in freedom of religion, his expectations are that he will not be hassled about religion at work.

Speaking Up

Loc Nam

| 0 | 1 | 2 | 3 | 4 | 5 | 6 | 7 | 8 | 9 | 10 |

You should speak your mind, express your views, and blow your own horn.

Good work will automatically be recognized and rewarded.

Speaking up...

In team meetings, some members try to boost their own image by talking about the outstanding job they are doing. On the other hand, Loc Nam never brings up his accomplishments, even when they are extraordinary. His cultural expectations are that any good work will automatically be recognized and need not be publicized.

Stereotypes

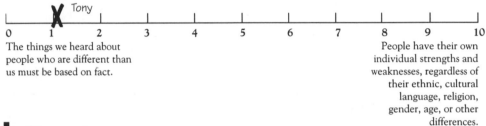

Tony

| 0 | 1 | 2 | 3 | 4 | 5 | 6 | 7 | 8 | 9 | 10 |

The things we heard about people who are different than us must be based on fact.

People have their own individual strengths and weaknesses, regardless of their ethnic, cultural language, religion, gender, age, or other differences.

Stereotypes...

Tony feels that certain groups of people take longer to learn their jobs than others. When he sees that Darnell will be a Tester on his team, Tony decides he will try to pass his work on to the other Tester until Darnell comes up to speed. Darnell is disappointed because his expectation is that he will be treated the same as any other team member.

Clearly, in the team process, sharing goals and finding commonalities are vital. However, to make your team function smoothly, you need to recognize the importance of understanding the principal forces impacting a diverse team. Learn as much as you can about others, and appreciate differences in values, perceptions, and expectations.

CHAPTER FIVE WORKSHEET: UNDERSTANDING DIVERSITY ISSUES WITHIN YOUR TEAM

1. What has been the impact of diversity *(or what future impact do you anticipate)* as your team progresses through the different phases of team development? Jot down specific examples.

Phase 1: Striving—Impact of diversity

_____

_____

_____

_____

Phase 2: Driving—Impact of diversity

_____

_____

_____

_____

_____

Phase 3: Thriving—Impact of diversity

_____

_____

_____

_____

Phase 4: Arriving—Impact of diversity

_____

_____

_____

_____

Phase 5: Reviving—Impact of diversity

_____

_____

_____

_____

2. Using the *Values, Perceptions, and Expectations Assessment* form in the Appendix, have each team member *"pair up"* and compare themselves with at least one other member of the team, using elements from the Values, Perceptions, and Expectations continuums they wish to explore with other team members. Have team members present and discuss their conclusions at the next team meeting.

DEVELOP SKILLS THAT MAKE A DIFFERENCE

With the understanding and appreciation you have gained about differences in others, you are now ready to learn about interpersonal skills that will enable you and your team members to capitalize on the team's diverse makeup.

♦ First, you need a strategy to communicate with other team members in a meaningful way, without letting differences become distractions. Communicating is a two-way process and you have to take an active role, whether sending or receiving messages.

♦ A second skill you need to develop involves recognizing and checking assumptions, both your own and those of others.

♦ A third valuable skill is the ability to resolve conflicts, particularly those having diversity elements in which values, perceptions, and expectations often play a major role.

Developing these skills will bring added value to your team.

Communication—Attentive Listening And Responding

Communication is a very complex process, and this guidebook looks at it primarily from the perspective of a diverse team.

All communication takes a speaker, a listener, and a medium through which the message is transmitted. Whether you are the speaker or the listener, you come to this experience with your own perceptions, assumptions, background, and attitudes. Keep in mind that other parties bring their *"baggage"* to the communication process as well.

Speaker   Message...   **Listener**

So much of any communication exchange is taken for granted that often little thought is applied to it. Here are some pointers that can help you develop a strategy when communicating with diverse team members.

➢ Don't just focus on the message; pay attention to the messenger too. Although the message is foremost, the messenger may be different from you, in looks, accent, and behavior, and these differences may affect how the message is formulated and delivered. Your perception of the messenger will probably also affect the way you interpret their message.

➢ Show interest in the other person by paying full attention. Purposely avoid distractions, whether internal *(unrelated thoughts, daydreams, etc.)* or external *(noise, unpleasant surroundings, physical discomfort, etc.)*.

Check for Understanding

As a speaker:

- Clarify the purpose of the communication.

- Make the message clear and concise.

- Be sure that no misinterpretation exists.

- Follow up with open-ended questions to assure that the listener has understood. ("Do you understand?" is not enough.)

As a listener:

- Pay close attention.

- Acknowledge the message by paraphrasing it and/or repeating it, as appropriate.

- Respond in a non-judgmental way.

Bob knew that he...

and Severina had miscommunicated before, so he had learned to improve his communication skills to make sure his message was clear and unambiguous. This morning he wanted to talk to her about the need to look at some potential changes in the assembly process that would affect Severina's job as well. *"I need to talk to you about some possible changes in assembly, and before any decisions are made, make sure all team members know what the effects are for everyone on the team,"* he began. *"So I want to ask you what you think the changes would mean for the Testers."*

Severina appreciated Bob's clarity, as he sometimes tended to jump ahead of himself without telling others what he was really asking or why. *"You mean the changes aren't yet a done deal, and you want to know what the implications would be for Darnell and me?"* paraphrased Severina. *"Right,"* replied Bob. *"Well, whether or not I agree with the proposed changes, here's what I see as the impact for us here in testing."*...

In addition to the speaker and the listener, the third element of communication is the medium, which can be spoken, written, or non-verbal. Within a diverse team, the medium can bring additional interference, overriding the message itself. In a one-on-one exchange, where both parties are face-to-face, you risk garbling the message by non-verbal cues, such as voice intonation, or eye contact, gestures, and various other types of body language.

In telephone conversations, remember that accents, interruptions, silence, and abruptness can distort the message.

In written communication using memos, faxes, or e-mail, avoid showing disrespect by using words with double meanings or culturally-offensive and insulting language. Keep in mind that in many cases, there will be a permanent record of what you write.

Effective communication in a diverse team requires that you think before you speak and listen attentively when the other party speaks. While diversity may introduce some interference, your communication skills can overcome the interference and build and strengthen relationships. Openness, sensitivity to others, and the willingness to look for commonalities can make a difference.

Responses

Some responses can help clarify the messages and avoid misinterpretation. Here are a few which you may find helpful:

"If I understand you correctly..."

"In other words..."

"Sounds like you..."

"So, you're saying..."

"So you think..."

"My sense is..."

"So your main concern is..."

"You feel..."

Checking Assumptions

Along with developing attentive listening and responding skills, you also need to be aware of assumptions which affect communication, and continually check them as they arise. Assumptions, when not examined, invariably block honest and open communication, affect behavior, and have an impact on team performance.

During a bull session with the guys...

Bob mentions that his younger brother Jim is unemployed and desperately needs work to support his family of five. Bob had tried to get Jim a job at Chester Cylinder, but was told that there were no openings. Bob complains about how unfair this is, saying, *"There are four women on our team and I'm sure they probably don't need jobs as much as Jim does."* He blames management for hiring too many women.

Someone points out that of the four women, two are single parents, one has a disabled husband, and the other lost most of her possessions in a disastrous house fire. Their needs are no less than Jim's. Actually, Bob's assumption was incorrect....

Examples of assumptions which have come up in other teams

- Soft-spoken people are timid, insecure, or not with it
- Some people with accents are perceived as uneducated or not so smart
- Women are too emotional
- Some groups are hard-working and smart while others are lazy
- Some people get jobs they're not qualified for
- Red-heads are hot-tempered
- Computer types are nerds
- The job of secretary is only for females
- White people think they're superior

In order to challenge your assumptions and remain open-minded, you will find the following points helpful:

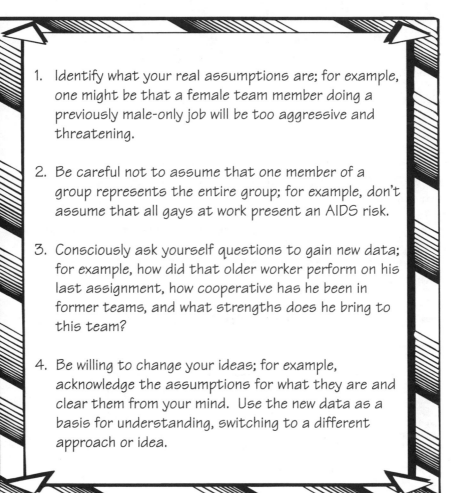

1. Identify what your real assumptions are; for example, one might be that a female team member doing a previously male-only job will be too aggressive and threatening.

2. Be careful not to assume that one member of a group represents the entire group; for example, don't assume that all gays at work present an AIDS risk.

3. Consciously ask yourself questions to gain new data; for example, how did that older worker perform on his last assignment, how cooperative has he been in former teams, and what strengths does he bring to this team?

4. Be willing to change your ideas; for example, acknowledge the assumptions for what they are and clear them from your mind. Use the new data as a basis for understanding, switching to a different approach or idea.

Challenging your assumptions, and doing something about them, will not come easily. Indeed, it's like driving a car with power steering up a mountain on a winding road. It feels comfortable, and takes only minor effort and minimal attention. If the power steering goes out, everything changes. Now you must pay complete attention and apply special effort. In challenging and changing your assumptions, you shed your *"power steering assumptions"* and develop new skills.

Conflict Resolution

Conflict resolution is a very broad topic which can be applied not only in business, but to everyday living as well. However, conflict resolution within diverse teams deserves special attention.

Whenever people work together, conflict is inevitable but often side-stepped. Misunderstandings are pushed inward or ignored. This can lead to strained team relationships and the goal then becomes learning to deal constructively with conflict.

In a diverse team, where cultural backgrounds differ, it is more important than ever that people understand that disputants respond differently to conflict. The more this element is appreciated, the healthier the resolution of the conflict can be.

On the other hand, when misunderstandings are escalated, conflict becomes even more severe. You can benefit if you recognize the diverse ways that other team members might handle a conflict situation. You can try to look at changing from your tightly-held positions to exploring new options, and not become emotional.

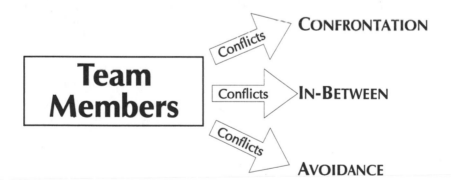

There seemed to be something behind Gordon's...
sarcastic comment directed at Loc Nam at the Monday morning meeting. *"Some people like to look like stars by putting in a lot of overtime—maybe they don't care about anything else. At least I have my priorities straight!"* Loc Nam was clearly offended and taken aback, but when he started to respond, Lucy jumped in before things escalated. *"Hey guys, let's cool off and take a look at what's going on here, before this gets any bigger than it needs to be."*...

Be prepared to deal with diversity-based conflict. Understand that some groups were raised to believe that direct confrontation is the way to deal with conflict, while others have learned that avoidance is the best way. Many cultures take positions between these extremes. These responses to conflict are best described as *"Conflict Resolution Styles"* which can take several forms.

Conflict Resolution Styles

The *"Avoider"* prefers to bypass or postpone a conflict and suppresses personal feelings or needs. Nothing is resolved and both parties come out losers.

The *"Competitor"* likes to win at all costs, strives to gain control, and is often motivated by a desire for power. The usual result is that the Competitor wins; the other party loses.

The *"Adaptor"* is willing to compromise and conform to the wishes and needs of the other party, surrendering personal considerations and giving in. The Adaptor loses and allows the other person to win.

The *"Cooperator"* acknowledges other points of view, explores all options, looks at creative alternatives, and works with the other party toward a mutually acceptable agreement. When this style is used, both parties can win.

Keep in mind that in some cases, any one of the Conflict Resolution Styles may produce the best results. For example, the problem may correct itself with time, and the Avoider in essence actually handled the situation most effectively.

On diverse teams, Conflict Resolution Styles are affected by cultural background and other differences. For example, different cultures believe conflict should be resolved:

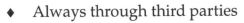

- ◆ Always through third parties
- ◆ Only by authority figures
- ◆ Through the hierarchical structure
- ◆ Entirely on the basis of trust
- ◆ Based on keeping harmonious relationships
- ◆ Assuring that disputants save face

For the most part, the examples shown above do not reflect the conventional Western approach to conflict resolution, but allow for a broad range of style differences. Know your own style. Think of it as an assessment instrument and determine what is important to you. Knowing how you deal with conflict and the fact that it may be very different from how others on your team deal with conflict should be helpful.

Putting Conflict Resolution Styles to work

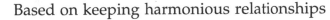

- ◆ Know that all styles can work at one time or another.
- ◆ Think about the members on your team and the styles they might be using.
- ◆ Recognize that their styles may be different than yours.
- ◆ Go in with patience and an open mind.
- ◆ Be willing to move away from your original position and explore all options.

Six Steps To Conflict Resolution

This six-step model can help you resolve a conflict.

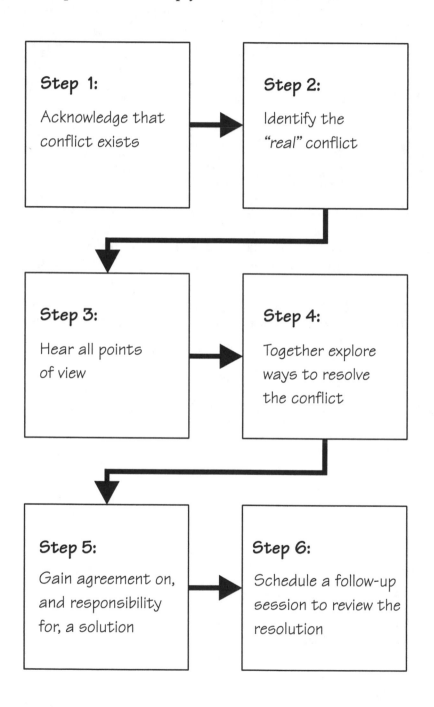

Step 1:

Acknowledge that conflict exists

Step 2:

Identify the "real" conflict

Step 3:

Hear all points of view

Step 4:

Together explore ways to resolve the conflict

Step 5:

Gain agreement on, and responsibility for, a solution

Step 6:

Schedule a follow-up session to review the resolution

Step 1: Acknowledge that conflict exists

If you don't address conflict immediately, it will heat up until it boils over. Then it becomes a surefire obstacle to your team's success. If you acknowledge that it exists and take steps to resolve it, you should be able to turn conflict into an opportunity.

"You have a point" said Gordon in reply to Lucy's ...

comment. *"This is about my view that it's not fair that Loc Nam puts in lots of overtime, while I have family and personal priorities that limit how much time I can put in. I feel this makes him look like a better candidate for promotion than me, and there is nothing I can do about it,"* said Gordon. *"And I don't think Gordon is being fair,"* Loc Nam responded, *"So yes, we do have a conflict."* ...

Whether you're a team member involved in a conflict, or a team leader or member observing a conflict, you must acknowledge the conflict before you can resolve it.

Step 2: Identify the *"real"* conflict

This step often requires diligent detective work. Identifying the real conflict is more difficult than it seems. Conflicts arise from both core issues and emotional issues.

In every conflict, there is interplay between these two kinds of issues. Even if the main conflict is about how to do something, emotional issues such as a threat to self-esteem or an outbreak of jealousy can intensify the conflict.

In diverse teams, the issues underlying a conflict often go beyond the situation at hand, back to differences in values, perceptions, and expectations. Getting to these underlying issues will help put the conflict resolution process on track.

> ## Lucy took the lead in identifying the "real" conflict...
> *"Don't you remember a few weeks ago when we compared each other's values, perceptions, and expectations, we were all different in some ways? I think that's what this is about—differences. One of the things we agreed to in that meeting was to focus on these differences to help avoid misunderstandings and jumping to conclusions. Remember?"...*

Once you've identified the underlying issues, the perspectives and points of view regarding the conflict need to be put on the table.

Perceptions ≠ Reality

Step 3: Hear all points of view

To successfully resolve conflict, you must understand both sides of the issue. Encourage team members who may be timid or unhappy to express themselves. Check for understanding and avoid debates over who is right or wrong.

In addition, discuss how the conflict is affecting people's performance. Focus on facts and behaviors, not feelings or personalities. The act of *"blaming"* causes emotions to become the center of attention. To avoid blaming, help team members identify similarities rather than differences. Emphasizing similarities allows both sides to meet on common ground.

"What's your perspective, Loc Nam?"...

asked Lucy. *"Well, if we put aside for now the point of whether or not putting in more overtime changes our chances for promotion, I can give you my point of view,"* Loc Nam replied. *"Yes, Gordon, I do put in a lot of overtime, and I'm doing it for the same reasons you are not—for my family. In my culture, the man's obligation is to provide everything he possibly can for his family, and he is expected to make a lot of sacrifices to do so. Sometimes, I'd rather to be at the park, or at a soccer game with my kids on the weekend, instead of working, but I was brought up to believe my first duty to my family is to work and be the provider. So, that's why I put in all the overtime I can, not to get a promotion. As a matter of fact, if I was offered a promotion, I'd probably not take it, because then I wouldn't be able to earn extra overtime pay."*

"Gordon, what about you?" asked Lucy. *"Okay, now I see Loc Nam's point of view,"* replied Gordon. *"I guess I was just looking at my side of things, and I shouldn't have said what I did. But what about the question of whether overtime counts towards our chances for a promotion? I would like to sort that out."*...

Once the different points of view have been aired *(including those of team members not directly involved in the conflict)*, it's time to come up with ideas to resolve the conflict.

Step 4: Together explore ways to resolve the conflict

It is important to explore each person's position, open up channels of communication, and involve others. An open discussion can result in a broadening of the information and alternatives available, and can lead to more trusting and healthy relationships between the people involved.

"Who else has some ideas on how to address...

Gordon and Loc Nam's issue?" Lucy asked the rest of the team. "Well, I think they both understand each other's position now, and that's further ahead than just a few minutes ago," commented Doris. "Yeah, that's three-quarters of the solution right there," added Roger. "Is there anything else they, or the team can suggest to get them the rest of the way?"...

With that the team brainstormed possible options on the meeting room blackboard.

> ◆ Loc Nam could work less overtime
>
> ◆ Gordon could work more overtime
>
> ◆ They could both continue as they are
>
> ◆ The team could clarify the relationship between overtime and promotions

Now that team members have discussed ways to resolve the conflict, it's time to lock in a solution, which is exactly what the next step does.

Step 5: Gain agreement on, and responsibility for, a solution

You can help members work together to solve the problem. All team members need to be as comfortable as possible with the solution. This must be a joint problem-solving session; no one should tell the other(s) how to solve the problem. You can't force agreement.

Gordon and Loc Nam agreed...

that they would both continue to schedule their overtime to meet their own individual needs and availability, and agreed that they understood each other's approach to overtime scheduling. The team also agreed to approach Personnel to get a clear policy decision on whether the amount of overtime worked was to be taken into consideration in promotion decisions. Lucy volunteered to go to Personnel, but Gordon and Loc Nam suggested they would be happy to go together instead. The team agreed....

Step 6: Schedule a follow-up session to review the resolution

And finally, let's turn to the last step in conflict resolution—evaluating its success. When team members know they're going to be held accountable for carrying out a commitment, they are far more likely to honor that commitment.

"Here's what Personnel said"...

began Gordon as he and Loc Nam got back to the team on the question of the relationship between overtime worked and consideration for promotion. After reporting to the team on what they learned from Personnel, the team agreed that all team conflicts should be handled with the same six-step approach. *"That way, we can get to the bottom of things, and come up with a solution, before the whole team feels the consequences of a conflict,"* pointed out Doris as the team got its regular meeting underway.

This chapter has been about developing skills for members of a diverse team to improve the way they work together. Developing these skills is always challenging, and even more so when diversity is taken into consideration.

Communication always contains interference. To overcome diversity interference, you can develop your listening and responding skills, put them to work, and make a difference in your team's performance.

Don't let your assumptions get in the way of how you relate to your fellow team members. Question your assumptions, eliminate the false ones, and move ahead with a clean slate.

When conflicts arise, recognize the cultural elements involved, factor them into the resolution process, build sensitivity, and create positive kinship.

CHAPTER SIX WORKSHEET: DEVELOPING SKILLS THAT MAKE A DIFFERENCE

1. Which of the following clarifying responses have you used when communicating with a team member?

- ☐ So, you're saying...
- ☐ In other words...
- ☐ So you think...
- ☐ My sense is...
- ☐ If I understand you correctly...
- ☐ So your main concern is...
- ☐ Sounds like you... , or looks like...
- ☐ It's interesting that...
- ☐ You feel...

2. Who have you observed in the workplace *(or elsewhere)* who is an effective communicator?

_____

_____

_____

_____

_____

_____

_____

3. What techniques of the effective commuicators you listed in
Question # 2 can you adopt to make you a better communicator
in your team setting?

_____

_____

_____

_____

_____

_____

4. What is your most frequently used conflict resolution style?

☐ Avoider

☐ Competitor

☐ Adapter

☐ Cooperator

5. When is this style not appropriate? Which style would you
adapt to in this situation?

_____

_____

_____

_____

REINFORCE THE TEAM NORMS

Every successful high performance team operates with a set of norms—that is, rules and practices guiding the way teams generally function. For a particular team, they are the basic standards of conduct and are usually unwritten. Your team will have its own norms; the positive ones should be constantly reinforced.

Examples of positive norms are:

+ All team members are involved in setting goals

+ Constructive team practices are understood and accepted

+ Everyone's roles and responsibilities are acknowledged

+ Members believe in working cooperatively and supporting each other

There can also be negative team norms. Some examples are:

- Off-color and demeaning jokes are acceptable

- Older people are ignored

- Accents are mocked

- Gays are shunned

Successful diverse teams also work under norms, but require additional positive ones relating to diversity. Some examples are:

✏ The team recognizes the importance of dealing with diversity

✏ Team members are comfortable with the topic of diversity

✏ Disagreements are to be non-judgmental

✏ Other persons' values are understood and appreciated

✏ Stereotypes are not allowed to interfere with team operation

✏ Members are especially careful not to leap to conclusions when interpersonal problems arise

✏ People share in each others' accomplishments and celebrate jointly, even developing symbols, ceremonies, and traditions.

The team strives to improve itself continually and uses tools such as the Diversity Self-Assessment Planner and the Team Diversity membership.

Note: Accommodating diverse points of view can end up creating new norms.

"You have a point," said Gordon ...

"This conflict is about my view that it's not fair that Loc Nam puts in a lot of overtime, while I have family and personal priorities that limit how much time I can put in. I feel this makes him look like a better candidate for promotion than me, and there is nothing I can do about it."...

Norms reflect the way things are expected to happen. They have unofficially evolved from the early days of the team, become embedded in the team character, and have been accepted by the members.

A team also operates under ground rules, which are like norms but more specific. Ground rules are usually in writing and are formally adopted by the team.

Establish Team Ground Rules

Diverse teams, because of their nature, have an obligation to address diversity through specific ground rules. These rules are needed to create an environment in which people of different backgrounds can understand one another and work toward the team goals. Consider some of the following for your team's ground rules:

✏ Realize that our team's diversity is one of our strengths, and we need to nurture it

✏ Make communication open and honest; minimize interruptions

✏ Respect team members as individuals

✏ Recognize that people may approach problems differently; listen and consider other points of view

✏ Make provisions for a forum to discuss and resolve diversity issues, when needed

✏ Remember that off-color and demeaning jokes are totally unacceptable and that diverse team members are not to be insulted

✏ Encourage new ideas

When establishing ground rules, all members of the team must be in agreement. Changes, or the adoption of new ground rules, must also be agreed to by everyone.

> ## *"Let's see if we can get our norms and ground rules...*
> *in writing, so we are all clear on what they are,"* stated Roger, as the team began a meeting scheduled specifically for that purpose. *"And new team members will know what's expected from day one,"* added Juan. *"I'll jot our brainstormed list of norms on the blackboard,"* Darnell volunteered. *"Once we agree on those, we can come up with the ground rules."* ...

Our Team Norms

✔ Our team values its diversity and recognizes it as one of our greatest strengths.

✔ Team members acknowledge and value each others' unique perspectives, values, and expectations.

✔ "Teamwork" means not only contributing work effort to the team goals, but contributing and sharing different ideas, perspectives, and expectations as well.

✔ The team recognizes that the type of support each member brings to the team will be different.

✔ The team recognizes that a diverse team make-up will present challenges, and agrees that all members share a responsibility to help overcome these challenges as they arise.

Our Team Ground Rules

✗ The team will assess itself every six months using the Team Diversity Assessment questionnaire.

✗ New team members, during their first week on the team, will interview each current team member to ask how the team norms play a role in the team's day-to-day operations.

✗ Team members will compare and discuss their own values, perceptions, and expectations with all team members. Time is included at every second team meeting to make this happen.

✗ All team members accept responsibility for playing a role in conflict resolution.

✗ In our day-to-day communication with each other, we will all make an extra effort to make sure we are focusing on both the message and the messenger.

Practice What You Preach

This section calls for you to practice what you preach, to turn words into actions. Because you're dealing with topics such as values, perceptions, and expectations, it will not be easy; however, it can be done. One of the most serious tests of the strength of the team norms occurs when new members join.

Let's look at an example of team norms to see what happens in one situation.

Without a full understanding of the norms, a new member can offend other members without even realizing it. For example, a new team member could come from a culture in which heavy perfume in the workplace is the accepted norm. Accordingly, she might come to work heavily perfumed, with no idea she is making others uncomfortable. Without realizing it, she could seriously upset a team member who has an allergy.

If this bothers you, it would be up to you to use the communication skills from the earlier chapters in this guidebook to help the new member understand the team norms and the reasons she will have to change. In other words, don't just stand there, do something!

Let's look at an example of ground rules to see what happens in another situation.

One team member unknowingly makes a derogatory comment about a new member from a different country, a clear violation of the ground rules. As an active group member, you have to address the individual who overstepped the rules, first by checking assumptions, and then by bringing your communication skills into play. Again, you have to put into practice the skills that deal with violations of ground rules.

Implementing the ground rules calls for a special effort by all team members.

- Introduce ground rules in the orientation process

- All members have the right to intervene in case of infractions of ground rules

- Prepare to use learned skills to correct violations

- Get comfortable with new concepts

- Post the ground rules as constant reminders

- All members should be encouraged to point out positive examples of other members following the ground rules

Ahmed, during his first week as a member...

of the team, was impressed with the attention the team gave to supporting the role of team member diversity as a team strength. He interviewed all but one of the team members and got their insights and examples of how the team capitalized on its diversity. He was told how the norms were lived on a day-to-day basis and how the team's ground rules played a key role in making things work.

When he had lunch with a couple of colleagues from his former department a few days after starting with the new team he summed up his impressions as follows, *"It's one thing to talk a good story about diversity and teamwork, but these guys actually do something to make it all work. They even have guidelines to make sure the team doesn't forget its commitment to teamwork and diversity. It's a great feeling!"...*

Check that actions on behalf of diversity become an everyday habit of team life. When this is accomplished, the team may be tempted to put the matter of diversity on *"automatic pilot."* But successful diverse teams are always on the alert for signs of reverting back to the old ways. If so, you must be prepared to go into the *"Reviving"* mode and reinforce the ground rules, with everyone's support.

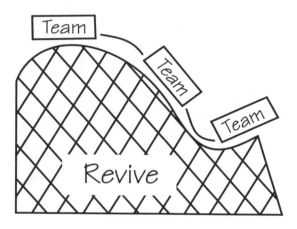

It is clearly impossible to include in the team norms or ground rules a solution or response to every possible diversity situation which may arise. There will be concerns which have not been anticipated, or which are so specific that they cannot be otherwise covered. In these cases, you should be able to apply common sense solutions, being careful to follow the spirit of the norms and ground rules.

In other words, a self-policing process is a good way to handle many diversity situations.

CHAPTER SEVEN WORKSHEET:
REINFORCE THE TEAM NORMS

1. What, if any, are your team's formal ground rules?

_____

_____

_____

_____

_____

_____

2. What are the team's informal norms?

_____

_____

_____

_____

_____

3. Which, of these informal norms, if any, need to be incorporated into the team's ground rules?

_____

_____

_____

_____

_____

_____

4. What other norms or ground rules need to be formally adopted by the team to ensure it can fully capitalize on its members' diversity?

_____

_____

_____

_____

_____

_____

_____

_____

5. How will the team's diversity norms be reinforced?

_____

_____

_____

_____

_____

_____

_____

_____

_____

_____

_____

_____

_____

_____

_____

_____

CHAPTER EIGHT

SUMMARY

You have seen how the addition of diversity to a high performance team changes the dynamics of the group. You have learned what diversity is and examined the effects of diversity on different types of teams and team structure.

Through self-assessment and team analysis, you were able to find areas where cultural barriers impaired team performance, and you determined how well you and your team currently address diversity.

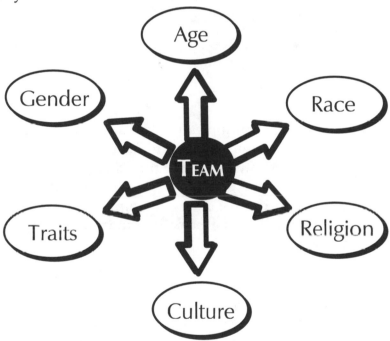

The message is clear. Your diverse team is now ready to take a proactive stance.

By building awareness, you will recognize what is important to you as an individual, as well as your personal values, perceptions, and expectations. Getting to know something about yourself is the first step in preparing to interact with people from diverse backgrounds. The same awareness is expected of your fellow team members.

By understanding the forces impacting a diverse team, you will understand the part that values, perceptions, and expectations play in team performance, that is, the role of *"differences."* In the team process, sharing goals and finding commonalities are vital, but at the same time you need to recognize there are special forces which affect diverse teams.

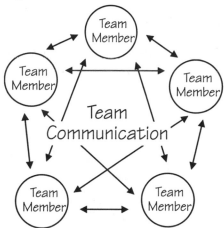

By developing strategic communication skills, you can build and strengthen relationships. You can learn to focus on the message and not the messenger, show interest in the other person, and check for understanding both as a speaker and as a listener. If there is interference from the medium, effective communication skills will help you overcome it, which is especially important when diversity is involved.

By checking assumptions, you can learn that your deeply-felt assumptions about other people may be wholly untrue. Those incorrect assumptions will affect your communication with diverse team members. After checking the basis for your assumptions, you may discover new data and find that your assumptions have been without foundation. Then you can move to a new level of understanding.

By employing the six-step conflict resolution model, you can manage conflicts with team members, including those from diverse backgrounds. As an aid in the resolution process, you can also analyze both your own conflict resolution style and those of other team members.

By reinforcing team norms, you can concentrate on the team's basic standards of conduct, strengthening the positive ones. Team norms are useful in making the team into a cohesive group, so that all members understand what is expected of them even though the norms are usually unwritten. Ground rules, usually written, are especially important in diverse teams because they can be constructed to anticipate diversity issues and resolve them.

There is no question that diversity has become a major element in today's work force. Teams, because of their unique structure, find that the way they cope with diversity can have far-reaching consequences.

Learning to handle diversity issues can be hard work. Is it worth it? You bet it is!

REPRODUCIBLE FORMS
AND WORKSHEETS

The pages in the Appendix are provided for you to photocopy and use appropriately.

VALUES, PERCEPTIONS, AND EXPECTATIONS ASSESSMENT

Values
The Work Ethic

```
|    |    |    |    |    |    |    |    |    |    |
0    1    2    3    4    5    6    7    8    9    10
```

Work is a major part
of who I am and I
dedicate myself to it
first and foremost.

My personal and family life
define who I am and take
priority
over work.

View Of Authority

```
|    |    |    |    |    |    |    |    |    |    |
0    1    2    3    4    5    6    7    8    9    10
```

The boss alone should
make decisions about
how things are done and
who should do them.

The boss should ask for,
listen to, and act on the
ideas, inputs, and
suggestions of his/her staff.

Outlook On Age

```
|    |    |    |    |    |    |    |    |    |    |
0    1    2    3    4    5    6    7    8    9    10
```

Older people have very
set ideas about how
work should be done
and are not willing to
change.

Older people are a source
of information and should
be consulted for their
wisdom and advice.

Individualism

```
|    |    |    |    |    |    |    |    |    |    |
0    1    2    3    4    5    6    7    8    9    10
```

Achievements should be
recognized and rewarded on
an individual basis only.
The best team is one with
high-performing individuals.

Group success is much
more important than
individual success.

Feelings

```
|    |    |    |    |    |    |    |    |    |    |
0    1    2    3    4    5    6    7    8    9    10
```

It is completely appropriate for
individuals to express their true
feelings about others.

Personal feelings should be
kept to yourself. Face-
saving is more important
than self-expression.

Perceptions
Formality

```
L____|____|____|____|____|____|____|____|____|____J
0    1    2    3    4    5    6    7    8    9    10
```

In an organization, employees should show respect for others who have a higher level of authority. Work only within the chain-of-command.

The best approach to organizational and team success is to encourage people to interact comfortably on a personal level, regardless of position or title.

Geography And Accents

```
L____|____|____|____|____|____|____|____|____|____J
0    1    2    3    4    5    6    7    8    9    10
```

A person's place of origin and manner of speaking is a strong indication of their work habits.

A person's work habits are very individual, and have nothing to do with their place of origin or their accent.

Privacy And Space Issues

```
L____|____|____|____|____|____|____|____|____|____J
0    1    2    3    4    5    6    7    8    9    10
```

Getting the job done and the message across is more important than adjusting to other people's privacy and space needs.

Everyone has their own privacy and space needs, which should be understood and respected by everyone at all times.

Expectations

The Role Of Management In Front-Line Work

```
L____|____|____|____|____|____|____|____|____|____J
0    1    2    3    4    5    6    7    8    9    10
```

Management should not be performing the tasks of the front-line workers.

Management should be encouraged to roll up their sleeves and get involved in front-line work on a regular basis.

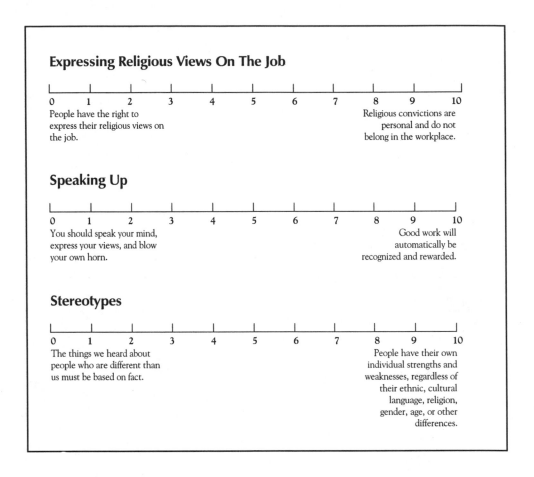

Expressing Religious Views On The Job

| | | | | | | | | | |
0   1   2   3   4   5   6   7   8   9   10

People have the right to express their religious views on the job.

Religious convictions are personal and do not belong in the workplace.

Speaking Up

| | | | | | | | | | |
0   1   2   3   4   5   6   7   8   9   10

You should speak your mind, express your views, and blow your own horn.

Good work will automatically be recognized and rewarded.

Stereotypes

| | | | | | | | | | |
0   1   2   3   4   5   6   7   8   9   10

The things we heard about people who are different than us must be based on fact.

People have their own individual strengths and weaknesses, regardless of their ethnic, cultural language, religion, gender, age, or other differences.

TEAM DIVERSITY ASSESSMENT

Check the appropriate box where (1) = Strongly disagree, (2) = Disagree, (3) = Neither agree or disagree, (4) = Agree, and
(5) = Strongly agree.

	1	2	3	4	5
1. Our team has a stated vision.					
2. The vision is accepted by all.					
3. The vision is understood by all.					
4. It includes reference to diversity.					
5. It considers the values and needs of each of its members.					
6. Our team environment supports diversity.					
7. Our team encourages members to be open with one another.					
8. Team members help one another.					
9. Our team promotes the sharing of success.					
10. Our team encourages individual interaction across diversity lines.					
11. The team members are open to differences of opinion.					
12. There is appreciation of the talents and skills of each individual.					
13. Members can count on one another, irrespective of their diverse backgrounds.					
14. The team is able to deal with interpersonal problems and conflicts.					
15. Team members feel secure in bringing up problems and conflicts.					
16. The team members can determine whether their problems are diversity-related.					
17. There is a system in place for addressing problems and conflicts.					

DIVERSITY SELF-ASSESSMENT PLANNER

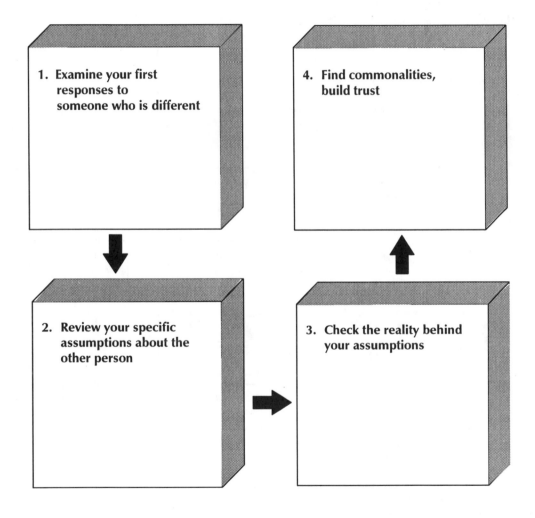

1. Examine your first responses to someone who is different

4. Find commonalities, build trust

2. Review your specific assumptions about the other person

3. Check the reality behind your assumptions

SELF-ASSESSMENT QUIZ

1. **A.** _____ My work has required me to deal with diverse groups of people, OR

   B. _____ I have always worked with people I consider to be like myself.

2. **A.** _____ I am interested in other languages and can communicate easily with limited English speakers, OR

   B. _____ I only know English and feel that it is completely up to the limited-English speakers to become competent in English.

3. **A.** _____ I reach out and am outgoing because I am interested in others, OR

   B. _____ I feel uncomfortable with people with disabilities.

4. **A.** _____ My first impressions of people are usually pretty accurate, OR

   B. _____ I realize that first impressions are not enough to judge a fellow team member.

5. **A.** _____ When people's names are unfamiliar to me I try to pronounce them correctly, OR

   B. _____ If someone's name is very unfamiliar to me, I suggest that I call them by a nickname that's shorter and easier than their own.

SELF-ASSESSMENT QUIZ (CONTINUED)

6. **A.** ____ I see nothing wrong with using words like *"girl," "boy," "honey,"* and *"babe,"* when referring to my co-workers, OR

   B. ____ I am aware that words like *"girl," "boy," "honey,"* and *"babe,"* may be offensive to some people.

7. **A.** ____ I believe that diverse employees must learn *"our ways"* quickly and fall in line right away, OR

   B. ____ I realize that diverse employees have different perspectives which can contribute greatly to the team.

8. **A.** ____ I believe that differences make it harder for people to work together, OR

   B. ____ I am willing to consider differences as a positive contribution to the team.

9. **A.** ____ I do not enjoy trying food or drinks that are unfamiliar, OR

   B. ____ I am open to all kinds of new food experiences.

10. **A.** ____ I am not comfortable being the *"only"* in a group setting, OR

    B. ____ I am aware that it is difficult to be the *"only"* in a group setting.

Professional And Personal Development Publications From Richard Chang Associates, Inc.

Designed to support continuous learning, these highly targeted, integrated collections from Richard Chang Associates, Inc. (RCA) help individuals and organizations acquire the knowledge and skills needed to succeed in today's ever-changing workplace. Titles are available through RCA, Jossey-Bass, Inc., fine bookstores, and distributors internationally.

Practical Guidebook Collection

Quality Improvement Series
Continuous Process Improvement
Continuous Improvement Tools, Volume 1
Continuous Improvement Tools, Volume 2
Step-By-Step Problem Solving
Meetings That Work!
Improving Through Benchmarking
Succeeding As A Self-Managed Team
Measuring Organizational Improvement Impact
Process Reengineering In Action
Satisfying Internal Customers First!

Management Skills Series
Interviewing And Selecting High Performers
On-The-Job Orientation And Training
Coaching Through Effective Feedback
Expanding Leadership Impact
Mastering Change Management
Re-Creating Teams During Transitions
Planning Successful Employee Performance
Coaching For Peak Employee Performance
Evaluating Employee Performance

High Performance Team Series
Success Through Teamwork
Building A Dynamic Team
Measuring Team Performance
Team Decision-Making Techniques

High-Impact Training Series
Creating High-Impact Training
Identifying Targeted Training Needs
Mapping A Winning Training Approach
Producing High-Impact Learning Tools
Applying Successful Training Techniques
Measuring The Impact Of Training
Make Your Training Results Last

Workplace Diversity Series
Capitalizing On Workplace Diversity
Successful Staffing In A Diverse Workplace
Team Building For Diverse Work Groups
Communicating In A Diverse Workplace
Tools For Valuing Diversity

Personal Growth And Development Collection

Managing Your Career in a Changing Workplace
Unlocking Your Career Potential
Marketing Yourself and Your Career
Making Career Transitions
Memory Tips For The Forgetful

101 Stupid Things Collection

101 Stupid Things Trainers Do To Sabotage Success
101 Stupid Things Supervisors Do To Sabotage Success
101 Stupid Things Employees Do To Sabotage Success
101 Stupid Things Salespeople Do To Sabotage Success
101 Stupid Things Business Travelers Do To Sabotage Success

About Richard Chang Associates, Inc.

Richard Chang Associates, Inc. (RCA) is a multi-disciplinary organizational performance improvement firm. Since 1987, RCA has provided private and public sector clients around the world with the experience, expertise, and resources needed to build capability in such critical areas as process improvement, management development, project management, team performance, performance measurement, and facilitator training. RCA's comprehensive package of services, products, and publications reflect the firm's commitment to practical, innovative approaches and to the achievement of significant, measurable results.

RCA Resources Optimize Organizational Performance

Consulting — Using a broad range of skills, knowledge, and tools, RCA consultants assist clients in developing and implementing a wide range of performance improvement initiatives.

Training — Practical, "real world" training programs are designed with a "take initiative" emphasis. Options include off-the-shelf programs, customized programs, and public and on-site seminars.

Curriculum And Materials Development — A cost-effective and flexible alternative to internal staffing, RCA can custom-develop and/or customize content to meet both organizational objectives and specific program needs.

Video Production — RCA's award-winning, custom video productions provide employees with information in a consistent manner that achieves lasting impact.

Publications — The comprehensive and practical collection of publications from RCA supports organizational training initiatives and self-directed learning.

Packaged Programs — Designed for first-time and experienced trainers alike, these programs offer comprehensive, integrated materials (including selected Practical Guidebooks) that provide a wide range of flexible training options. Choose from:

- Meetings That Work! ToolPAK™
- Step-By-Step Problem Solving ToolKIT™
- Continuous Process Improvement Packaged Training Program
- Continuous Improvement Tools, Volume 1 ToolPAK™
- Continuous Improvement Tools, Volume 2 ToolPAK™
- High Involvement Teamwork™ Packaged Training Program

RICHARD
CHANG
ASSOCIATES

World Class Resources. World Class Results.^{SM}

Richard Chang Associates, Inc.
Corporate Headquarters
15265 Alton Parkway, Suite 300, Irvine, California 92618 USA
(800) 756-8096 • (949) 727-7477 • Fax: (949) 727-7007
E-Mail: info@rca4results.com • www.richardchangassociates.com

U.S. Offices in Irvine and Atlanta • Licensees and Distributors Worldwide